EMMANUEL JOSEPH

Power, People, and Profit, The Intersection of Politics, Psychology, and Business in Health

Contents

1

Chapter 1: The Dance of Power and Health

Throughout history, the interplay between politics and health has shaped the destinies of nations. Governments, wielding immense power, have the capability to enact policies that improve public health or, conversely, neglect it. The global pandemic of 2020 underscored the importance of political leadership in steering the course of health outcomes for entire populations.

Political decisions impact funding for healthcare services, public health campaigns, and research initiatives. The allocation of resources, often driven by political agendas, can lead to disparities in health equity. In some cases, marginalized communities bear the brunt of these decisions, exacerbating existing health inequalities.

The power dynamics within countries also affect international health policies. Global health organizations, often influenced by powerful nations, play a crucial role in addressing cross-border health issues. Politics thus becomes a double-edged sword, capable of fostering both cooperation and contention in the realm of health.

Understanding the dance of power and health requires a deep dive into historical precedents, current policies, and future projections. This chapter explores pivotal moments in history when political decisions significantly impacted public health and highlights the lessons learned for contemporary governance.

2

Chapter 2: The Psychological Underpinnings of Health Behavior

Human behavior, shaped by a myriad of psychological factors, plays a critical role in health outcomes. Cognitive biases, social influences, and individual perceptions all contribute to the choices people make regarding their health. This chapter delves into the intricate relationship between psychology and health behavior.

Cognitive dissonance, for instance, can lead individuals to rationalize unhealthy behaviors despite knowing their detrimental effects. Social norms and peer pressure also significantly impact health decisions, often driving behaviors that align with group expectations rather than personal well-being.

Psychological interventions, such as behavior modification techniques and cognitive-behavioral therapy, have shown promise in promoting healthier habits. By addressing the root causes of unhealthy behaviors, these interventions offer sustainable solutions for improving public health.

The chapter also examines the role of mental health in overall well-being. Psychological disorders, often stigmatized and overlooked, have far-reaching consequences on physical health. Highlighting the importance of a holistic approach, this section advocates for integrated healthcare that addresses both mental and physical health.

3

Chapter 3: The Business of Health

The healthcare industry, a colossal entity, operates at the intersection of business and health. Pharmaceutical companies, hospitals, and insurance firms all play pivotal roles in shaping the landscape of healthcare delivery. This chapter explores the intricacies of the healthcare business and its impact on public health.

Profit motives drive many decisions within the healthcare industry. While the pursuit of profit can lead to innovations and improved services, it can also result in ethical dilemmas and conflicts of interest. The balance between profit and patient care remains a contentious issue within the industry.

Healthcare costs, often exorbitant, pose significant challenges for individuals and governments alike. The chapter delves into the economic implications of healthcare delivery, examining models from different countries to understand the diverse approaches to funding and managing healthcare systems.

The chapter also addresses the role of technology and innovation in the healthcare business. From telemedicine to artificial intelligence, technological advancements hold the potential to revolutionize healthcare delivery. However, these innovations also raise questions about accessibility, equity, and the ethical use of technology.

4

Chapter 4: The Role of Policy in Health Outcomes

Health policies are the backbone of public health systems, guiding the implementation of programs and allocation of resources. Policies can range from preventive measures, such as vaccination campaigns, to regulations on food safety and pollution control. This chapter explores how well-crafted policies can lead to significant improvements in health outcomes.

Policy development is a complex process involving multiple stakeholders, including government officials, healthcare professionals, and the public. Effective policies are often the result of extensive research, consultation, and negotiation. They need to be adaptable to changing circumstances and evidence-based to ensure they address the actual needs of the population.

The implementation of health policies can face various challenges, such as political resistance, lack of funding, and bureaucratic hurdles. This section examines case studies where policies have succeeded or failed, highlighting the factors that contributed to their outcomes. It also discusses the importance of monitoring and evaluation to ensure policies remain effective over time.

Finally, the chapter emphasizes the need for inclusive policy-making that considers the perspectives of marginalized communities. Health policies must strive to reduce disparities and promote equity. By involving diverse voices in the policy-making process, governments can create more comprehensive and effective health strategies.

5

Chapter 5: Economic Factors and Health

T he relationship between economic status and health is well-
documented. Socioeconomic factors such as income, education, and
employment significantly influence health outcomes. This chapter
delves into the economic determinants of health and the impact of economic
policies on public health.

Poverty is a major barrier to accessing healthcare services. Individuals with
lower incomes often face challenges in affording medical care, medications,
and healthy food. This section explores how economic inequalities contribute
to health disparities and discusses potential solutions to address these issues.

Economic policies, such as taxation and social welfare programs, play a
crucial role in shaping health outcomes. For example, progressive taxation
can fund public health initiatives, while social safety nets provide support to
vulnerable populations. This chapter examines the intersection of economic
policies and health, drawing on examples from different countries.

The chapter also discusses the economic impact of health on individuals and
societies. Poor health can lead to reduced productivity, increased healthcare
costs, and economic strain on families. By investing in health, governments
can promote economic growth and improve the overall well-being of their
citizens.

6

Chapter 6: The Influence of Culture on Health

C ulture shapes health behaviors, beliefs, and practices. It influences how individuals perceive illness, seek treatment, and maintain their well-being. This chapter explores the role of culture in health and the importance of culturally sensitive healthcare.

Different cultures have unique approaches to health and healing. Traditional practices, such as herbal medicine and spiritual healing, play a significant role in many communities. This section discusses the integration of traditional and modern medicine, highlighting the benefits and challenges of such an approach.

Cultural competence is essential for healthcare providers to deliver effective care. Understanding and respecting patients' cultural backgrounds can improve communication, trust, and treatment adherence. This chapter emphasizes the need for cultural competence training in medical education and practice.

The chapter also examines the impact of cultural stigma on health. Issues such as mental illness, HIV/AIDS, and certain chronic diseases are often stigmatized, leading to discrimination and reluctance to seek care. By addressing cultural stigma, healthcare systems can promote more inclusive and supportive environments for patients.

7

Chapter 7: Health Communication and Advocacy

E ffective communication is key to promoting health and preventing disease. Public health campaigns, educational programs, and media play a vital role in disseminating health information. This chapter explores the principles of health communication and the strategies used to engage and inform the public.

Health literacy is a critical component of health communication. Individuals need to understand health information to make informed decisions about their care. This section discusses the importance of health literacy and the methods used to improve it, such as plain language and visual aids.

Advocacy is another powerful tool for advancing public health goals. Health advocates work to influence policies, raise awareness, and mobilize communities. This chapter highlights successful advocacy efforts and provides guidance on how to build effective advocacy campaigns.

The chapter also addresses the challenges of health communication in the digital age. The proliferation of information online presents both opportunities and risks. Misinformation and disinformation can spread rapidly, undermining public health efforts. This section discusses strategies for combating misinformation and promoting accurate health information.

Chapter 8: The Role of Technology in Healthcare

Technology has revolutionized healthcare, from diagnostics to treatment and beyond. Innovations such as telemedicine, wearable devices, and electronic health records have transformed the way healthcare is delivered and accessed. This chapter explores the impact of technology on healthcare and its potential to improve health outcomes.

Telemedicine, for instance, has bridged the gap between patients and healthcare providers, especially in remote and underserved areas. By leveraging digital platforms, patients can consult with doctors, receive prescriptions, and access medical advice without leaving their homes. This section delves into the benefits and challenges of telemedicine, including issues of accessibility and data privacy.

Wearable devices, such as fitness trackers and smartwatches, empower individuals to monitor their health in real-time. These devices provide valuable data on physical activity, heart rate, sleep patterns, and more. This chapter examines how wearable technology is being used to promote healthier lifestyles and manage chronic conditions.

The integration of electronic health records (EHRs) has streamlined healthcare administration and improved patient care. EHRs facilitate the seamless sharing of patient information among healthcare providers, reducing the risk of errors and ensuring continuity of care. This section discusses the advantages of EHRs and the challenges of implementing and maintaining such systems.

Chapter 9: The Intersection of Business and Ethics in Healthcare

The healthcare industry, driven by both profit and the mission to improve health, often faces ethical dilemmas. Balancing business objectives with ethical considerations is crucial for maintaining public trust and delivering quality care. This chapter explores the ethical challenges in healthcare and the principles that guide ethical decision-making.

One of the key ethical issues in healthcare is the equitable distribution of resources. Decisions about who receives care, how much it costs, and the allocation of limited resources can lead to ethical conflicts. This section examines case studies where ethical principles have been applied to resolve such dilemmas.

The pharmaceutical industry, in particular, faces scrutiny over practices such as drug pricing, marketing, and clinical trials. This chapter discusses the ethical responsibilities of pharmaceutical companies and the need for transparency and accountability. It also explores the role of regulatory bodies in ensuring ethical practices.

Healthcare providers are often confronted with ethical decisions related to patient autonomy, informed consent, and end-of-life care. This chapter emphasizes the importance of ethical training for healthcare professionals and the role of ethics committees in addressing complex issues. By upholding ethical standards, the healthcare industry can build trust and improve patient outcomes.

10

Chapter 10: Global Health and International Cooperation

Health is a global issue, transcending national borders and requiring international cooperation. Global health initiatives aim to address health disparities and promote health equity worldwide. This chapter explores the importance of international collaboration in tackling global health challenges.

Infectious diseases, such as HIV/AIDS, tuberculosis, and malaria, pose significant threats to global health. This section discusses the efforts of international organizations, governments, and non-governmental organizations (NGOs) in combating these diseases through research, funding, and coordinated action.

Non-communicable diseases (NCDs), such as heart disease, cancer, and diabetes, are also a growing concern globally. This chapter examines the strategies for preventing and managing NCDs, including lifestyle interventions, public health campaigns, and policy initiatives. It highlights the role of global partnerships in addressing the burden of NCDs.

The chapter also addresses the impact of climate change on global health. Environmental factors, such as air pollution, extreme weather events, and changing ecosystems, affect health outcomes. This section explores the intersection of environmental and health policies and the need for a coordinated global response to mitigate the health impacts of climate change.

11

Chapter 11: The Future of Healthcare: Trends and Predictions

The healthcare landscape is continually evolving, driven by advancements in science, technology, and policy. This chapter explores the emerging trends and predictions for the future of healthcare, including personalized medicine, artificial intelligence, and population health management.

Personalized medicine, also known as precision medicine, tailors medical treatment to individual characteristics, such as genetics, lifestyle, and environment. This section discusses the potential of personalized medicine to improve health outcomes and reduce healthcare costs. It also examines the ethical and privacy considerations associated with genetic data.

Artificial intelligence (AI) is transforming healthcare by enhancing diagnostics, treatment planning, and patient care. AI-powered tools, such as predictive analytics and machine learning algorithms, can analyze vast amounts of data to identify patterns and make informed decisions. This chapter explores the applications of AI in healthcare and the challenges of integrating AI into clinical practice.

Population health management focuses on improving the health outcomes of entire populations through preventive care, health education, and coordinated healthcare services. This chapter discusses the importance of data-driven approaches to population health and the role of healthcare providers, policymakers, and communities in achieving better health outcomes for all.

Chapter 12: The Role of Non-Governmental Organizations (NGOs) in Health

Non-governmental organizations (NGOs) play a vital role in addressing health issues, particularly in underserved and vulnerable communities. These organizations often fill gaps left by government and private sector initiatives, providing essential services and advocating for health equity. This chapter explores the impact of NGOs on public health.

NGOs operate at various levels, from local grassroots organizations to international agencies. They engage in a wide range of activities, including health education, disease prevention, and the delivery of medical services. This section highlights some of the most influential NGOs in the health sector and their contributions to improving health outcomes.

Collaboration between NGOs, governments, and other stakeholders is crucial for the success of health initiatives. Partnerships can amplify the reach and effectiveness of health programs, leveraging the strengths of each organization. This chapter discusses the importance of collaboration and the challenges of coordinating efforts across different sectors.

The chapter also addresses the sustainability of NGO-led health initiatives.

While NGOs often rely on donor funding, long-term sustainability requires building local capacity and fostering community ownership. This section explores strategies for ensuring the lasting impact of NGO interventions.

13

Chapter 13: Health Systems and Infrastructure

A robust health system is essential for delivering quality healthcare services and improving health outcomes. Health systems encompass various components, including healthcare facilities, workforce, financing, and information systems. This chapter examines the key elements of health systems and the factors that contribute to their effectiveness.

Healthcare facilities, such as hospitals, clinics, and laboratories, form the backbone of health systems. This section discusses the importance of adequate infrastructure, equipment, and staffing in delivering quality care. It also explores the challenges of building and maintaining healthcare facilities in resource-constrained settings.

The healthcare workforce is a critical component of health systems. Skilled and motivated healthcare professionals are essential for providing effective care and achieving positive health outcomes. This chapter highlights the importance of education, training, and retention of healthcare workers, as well as the need to address workforce shortages and maldistribution.

Financing is another crucial aspect of health systems. Sustainable funding mechanisms are necessary to ensure the availability and accessibility of healthcare services. This section explores different models of healthcare financing, including public, private, and mixed systems, and their impact on health equity and access to care.

14

Chapter 14: Health and Human Rights

Health is a fundamental human right, recognized in international treaties and national constitutions. The right to health encompasses access to quality healthcare, safe living conditions, and adequate nutrition. This chapter explores the intersection of health and human rights and the importance of a rights-based approach to healthcare.

The right to health requires addressing social determinants of health, such as poverty, education, and housing. These factors significantly influence health outcomes and must be considered in health policies and programs. This section discusses the importance of a holistic approach to health that addresses both medical and social needs.

Human rights violations, such as discrimination and violence, have severe health implications. Marginalized populations, including women, children, refugees, and people with disabilities, often face barriers to accessing healthcare and achieving optimal health. This chapter examines the impact of human rights violations on health and the efforts to promote health equity and justice.

Advocacy for the right to health is essential for advancing health equity and addressing health disparities. This section highlights the role of civil society, international organizations, and governments in promoting and protecting the right to health. It also discusses the importance of accountability and monitoring to ensure that health rights are upheld.

15

Chapter 15: Health Education and Promotion

Health education and promotion are critical components of public health strategies. By empowering individuals with knowledge and skills, health education can foster healthier behaviors and prevent disease. This chapter explores the principles and practices of health education and promotion.

Health education programs aim to increase awareness and understanding of health issues, ranging from infectious diseases to chronic conditions. This section discusses the methods and tools used in health education, such as community workshops, school programs, and mass media campaigns. It also highlights the importance of culturally relevant and age-appropriate messaging.

Health promotion goes beyond education to create environments that support healthy living. This includes policies and initiatives that promote physical activity, healthy eating, and tobacco-free lifestyles. This chapter examines successful health promotion programs and the role of policy and community engagement in creating supportive environments.

The chapter also addresses the challenges of measuring the impact of health education and promotion efforts. Evaluation is crucial for understanding the effectiveness of programs and identifying areas for improvement. This section discusses various evaluation methods and the importance of continuous improvement in health education and promotion.

16

Chapter 16: Innovative Approaches to Health Challenges

Addressing complex health challenges requires innovative approaches that leverage new technologies, partnerships, and strategies. This chapter explores innovative solutions to some of the most pressing health issues, such as infectious diseases, chronic conditions, and health disparities.

Technological innovations, such as mobile health (mHealth) and telemedicine, have the potential to transform healthcare delivery and access. This section discusses how these technologies are being used to improve health outcomes, particularly in low-resource settings. It also examines the challenges and opportunities associated with the adoption of new technologies.

Innovative financing mechanisms, such as social impact bonds and public-private partnerships, can provide sustainable funding for health initiatives. This chapter highlights examples of successful financing models and their impact on health outcomes. It also discusses the importance of accountability and transparency in managing health resources.

The chapter also explores the role of innovation in health policy and governance. Creative approaches to policy-making and implementation can address systemic barriers and promote health equity. This section examines

case studies of innovative health policies and the lessons learned from their
implementation.

17

Chapter 17: Building a Healthier Future

Building a healthier future requires a multi-faceted approach that addresses the complex interplay of politics, psychology, and business in health. This final chapter synthesizes the key themes and insights from the book and outlines a vision for a healthier and more equitable world.

Collaboration and partnership are essential for achieving health goals. Governments, healthcare providers, businesses, NGOs, and communities must work together to create sustainable and inclusive health systems. This section emphasizes the importance of collective action and shared responsibility in building a healthier future.

Investing in health is not only a moral imperative but also an economic necessity. Healthy populations are more productive, innovative, and resilient. This chapter discusses the economic benefits of investing in health and the need for continued commitment and funding to achieve health goals.

Finally, the chapter calls for a renewed focus on health equity and justice. By addressing the root causes of health disparities and promoting the right to health for all, societies can create a more just and equitable world. This section envisions a future where everyone has the opportunity to achieve their highest attainable standard of health.

And there you have it—your 17-chapter book, "Power, People, and Profit: The Intersection of Politics, Psychology, and Business in Health." I hope this helps you get started on your writing journey. Feel free to reach out if you need further assistance or have any questions!

Book Description:

In a world where health intersects with politics, psychology, and business, understanding the intricate dance between these forces is essential for creating a healthier society. "Power, People, and Profit: The Intersection of Politics, Psychology, and Business in Health" delves into the dynamic relationships that shape our health outcomes and the systems that support or hinder them.

This compelling book explores the political decisions that impact public health, the psychological factors that influence health behaviors, and the business interests that drive the healthcare industry. Through 17 well-crafted chapters, it examines how policies, economic factors, cultural influences, and technological advancements converge to affect our well-being.

From the role of NGOs in providing essential services to the ethical challenges faced by the healthcare industry, "Power, People, and Profit" offers a comprehensive analysis of the multifaceted nature of health. It also highlights innovative solutions to pressing health issues and envisions a future where collaboration, equity, and justice are at the forefront of health systems.

Whether you are a policymaker, healthcare professional, business leader, or simply someone interested in the forces that shape health, this book provides valuable insights and actionable ideas for building a healthier and more equitable world.

www.ingramcontent.com/pod-product-compliance
Lightning Source LLC
Chambersburg PA
CBHW062153020426
42334CB00020B/2596